My Healthy Body

Eating

Veronica Ross

Chrysalis Children's Books

First published in the UK in 2002 by
Chrysalis Children's Books
An imprint of Chrysalis Books Group Plc
The Chrysalis Building, Bramley Road, London W10 6SP

ISBN 1 84138 405 4

British Library Cataloguing in Publication Data
for this book is available from the British Library.

Design: Bean Bog Frag Design
Picture researcher: Terry Forshaw
Consultant: Carol Ballard

Printed in China

10 9 8 7 6 5 4 3 2

(T) = Top, (B) = Bottom, (L) = Left, (R) = Right, (C) = Centre

Picture acknowledgements:
All Photography by Claire Paxton with the exception of: 5 © Digital
Vision; 6 (TR), (TCR), (BCR); 7 (TL), (TR), (CR), (BL), (BC); 8 (TL), (TR); 9 (TR),
(CL); 11 (CL), (BL); 12 (TR); 13 (TL), (TCL), (TCR), (BR); 14 (T), (B); 15 (TR), (C),
(BL); 17 (TR), (TC), (TCR), (BCL), 19 (TC), (TR); Chrysalis Images 20 ©
Bubbles/Ian West; 22 (BL) Chrysalis Images; 23 © Corbis/Earl &
Nazima Kowall; 24 (T) Chrysalis Images; 25 © Wellcome Photo
Library/Anthea Sieveking; 26 © Photo Disc/Ryan Mcvay; 27 (T) ©
Bubbles/Chris Miles, (B) Bubbles/Richard Yard; 29
(B) Chrysalis Images.

Contents

Why do I eat? 4

A balanced diet 6

Foods for growth 8

Energy foods 10

Fatty and oily 12

Food for health 14

Fantastic fibre 16

Drink up 18

Being a vegetarian 20

Food fabulous food 22

Food allergies 24

Preparing food 26

Bad habits 28

Words to remember 30

Index 32

Why do I eat?

Everyone needs to eat. Food helps you to stay healthy and gives you the energy you need to work and play. Food also protects you from illness and helps you to grow.

If you don't eat for a few hours, you will soon begin to feel very hungry.

Your body uses energy when you work and play, and when you're painting pictures!

You should try to eat three healthy meals each day.

A balanced diet

You need to eat lots of
different foods to stay healthy.
A well balanced diet includes
different types of foods that give
you all the goodness you need.

How many of these
foods can you name?
How many do you like to eat?

Fruit and vegetables are very good for you.

Your diet is the food and drink that you eat and drink every day.

Foods for growth

Meat, fish, milk, eggs, cheese, nuts, beans and cereals help you to grow. They also keep your body in good working order.

Eggs make you grow strong. Eat one for breakfast!

Growth foods help to repair broken bones.

The foods shown on these pages will build your muscles, bones and teeth.

Energy foods

Rice, bread, cereals, potatoes and pasta give you energy and keep you warm. You should try to eat some of these foods at every main meal.

Fruit also gives you energy.

Start the day with
a breakfast of
toast or cereal for
a burst of energy.

If you play lots of sport
you will need to eat
extra energy foods.

Fatty and oily

You only need to eat small amounts of fatty foods to keep fit and well. Fat is found in chocolate, butter, cheese, sardines, avocados and vegetable oil.

Fried foods, such as chips and samosas, contain a lot of fat.

Try not to eat too many chocolate bars, cakes and biscuits.

If you're feeling peckish between meals try to eat an apple or a banana instead of a biscuit.

Food for health

Different foods do different jobs. Vegetables and fruit give you healthy skin and blood, and help cuts to heal. Milk, cheese and yoghurt give you calcium, which keeps your bones strong.

Dark green vegetables, such as broccoli, are especially good for you.

Fish are packed with goodness. They will help you to grow.

A glass of milk every day will help keep your teeth healthy.

Oranges help your body fight off coughs and colds.

Fantastic fibre

Some foods, such as pasta, wholemeal bread and vegetables, contain fibre. Fibre helps your body use the food that you eat.

Foods rich in fibre make you feel very full.

Pasta, lentils, brown rice, wholemeal bread, fruit and vegetables contain fibre.

Fibre is found in plants, such as wheat.

Drink up

You could survive for quite a long time without food, but you would not live long without water. All the parts of your body need water.

Your body needs about two litres of water a day.

You need to drink more when it is hot. This is because you sweat more in hot weather, so you must replace the water you lose.

Water is found in fruit and vegetables as well as drinks.

Being a vegetarian

Vegetarians are people who do not eat meat. If you decide to become a vegetarian, you should eat a wide variety of fruit and vegetables, as well as beans, nuts, milk and cheese. These foods will give you all the goodness you need.

Most cafes have vegetarian food.

20

This meal of rice, salad and stuffed pepper is just as healthy as a meal that contains meat.

Make a picnic packed with tasty vegetarian food.

Some vegetarians do not like the taste of meat. Others believe that eating animals is wrong.

Food fabulous food

Food keeps us healthy, but eating a delicious meal is also very enjoyable! That's why we eat special foods when we celebrate birthdays, weddings or festivals. What are your favourite foods?

A birthday party wouldn't be the same without cake, biscuits and jelly.

A wedding
feast in Korea.

A large meal stays in your stomach
for more than three hours.

Food allergies

Some people are allergic
to certain foods. Milk, eggs, shellfish, strawberries,
peanuts and chocolate are all foods that can
cause a rash or stomachache.

Chocolate
may give
some people
a headache.

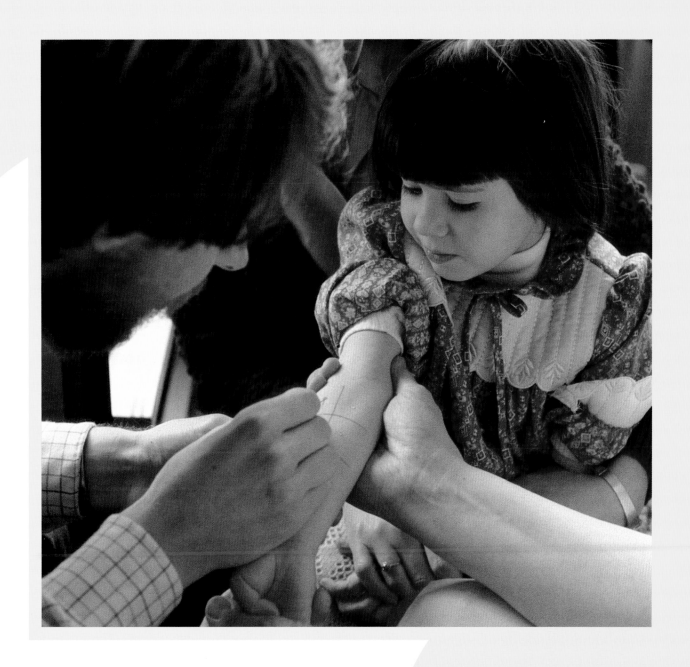

If you think you have a food allergy, your doctor may give you special tests to find out which food makes you feel ill.

Some foods have chemicals in them which give the food extra colour or taste. These may make some people feel ill.

preparing food

It's important to make sure that your hands are clean before you eat or pick food up. Keep fish, meat, cheese and milk in the fridge. Throw away food that is past its sell by date.

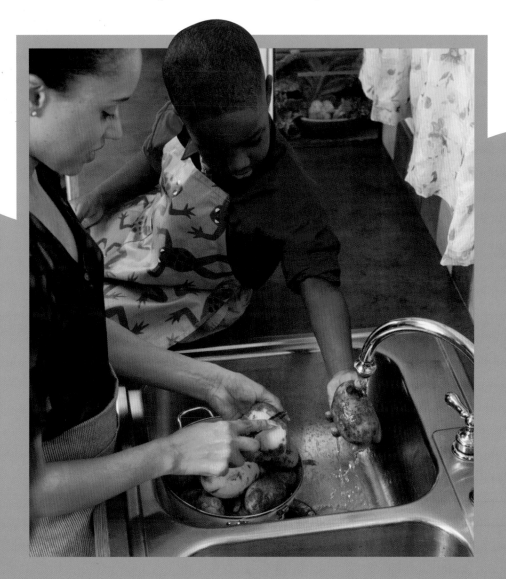

Always wash fruit and vegetables before you eat them.

Put on an apron before you start cooking.

When you have finished, wash your hands and tidy up!

Do not leave food uncovered, especially in hot weather.

Bad habits

Take-away foods, such as chips, hamburgers and donuts, are high in fat, sugar and salt. If you ate this type of food all the time you would soon become very unhealthy.

Too many sweet foods and fizzy drinks can make your teeth decay.

Burgers and chips taste great, but they are full of fat. Try not to eat them too often.

If you eat too much food in one go, you might feel sick!

Words to remember

allergy

A reaction to food or other things, such as dust or pollen.

blood

The red liquid that flows around your body.

bones

The hard parts inside your body that make up your skeleton.

calcium

The substance that your bones are made of.

decay

To go bad or to rot.

energy

The power you need to be able to work and play without feeling tired.

muscles
Bundles of soft, stretchy fibres inside your body that make you move.

protect
To look after.

repair
To mend.

samosas
Pastry snacks filled with meat or vegetables.

sweat
Water that comes from your skin when you are very hot.

wholemeal bread
Bread that is made with the whole grain.

Index

allergies 24, 25, 30

blood 14, 30
bones 9, 14, 30

calcium 14, 30

diet 6, 7

energy 4, 5, 10, 11,
   30

fatty foods 12, 13,
   28, 29
fibre 16, 17

growth foods 8, 9

muscles 9, 31

preparing food 26, 27

skin 14
special food 22, 23
sweat 19, 31

take-away food 28, 29
teeth 9, 15, 28

vegetarians 20, 21

water 18, 19